ABRAHAM RATTNER

ABRAHAM RATTNER

KENNEDY GALLERIES, INC.

Founded in 1874 by H. Wunderlich

20 EAST 56TH STREET

NEW YORK · NEW YORK 10022

Abraham Rattner is represented in numerous important collections of
contemporary art, both private and public, throughout the United States.

This catalogue was set in Univers by Cooper & Cohen, New York City.
Printed by offset in four color process by Ampco-Advertisers, Inc., New
York City, on Mead Moistrite Matte and Strathmore Grandee.

ABRAHAM RATTNER

Abraham Rattner has been exhibited, at the Whitney Museum, as ''An American Expressionist.'' On the other hand, he grew up, artistically, in a Paris dominated by Cubism and Surrealism and elements of both can be found in many of his paintings. A personal discovery was the aged Monet, still painting at Giverney, where Rattner lived briefly, and Impressionism, too, is recalled in the American's rich use of color. More strictly in terms of his own country, Rattner anticipated and thoroughly mastered many of the devices of Abstract Expressionism, or Action Painting, before those names existed. Moreover, he incorporated those devices into a complex and meaningful style of painting which easily survives the decline of Abstract Expressionism and which grows more beautiful, more reward-ing and more masterful as year follows year in a great artist's full and sustained maturity.

That maturity was, by contemporary standards, a long time coming. There were moments when Rattner himself doubted not so much that it would come as that, after devoting his entire young manhood to art, he would ever achieve recognition and acceptance and make a go of it in painting.

The elements that finally fused to make a mature artist out of an extremely talented practitioner are easily stated and even easily discerned in periods of his work, in certain subjects, in individual paintings and passages. Yet such analysis does not pretend to grasp the results of that fusion, the richness and resonance of the paintings, the force of their presence. As in all human achievement of this quality, the whole is greater than the sum of its parts.

The parts are as clear in the artist's life as they are in his work. The first, and artistically the foundation, is the immersion in French art when French art flowered in a glorious culmination of more than two centuries of steady growth. The goal of Louis XIV to make France the capital of art was brilliantly achieved in the Paris of the Third Republic, full of foreigners from all over who came to learn French art and to make it more extensive: Picasso and Miro from Spain, Lipchitz, Soutine, and Chagall from Eastern Europe, Modigliani and di Chirico from Italy, and, from America, Abraham Rattner.

Rattner went to Paris when the going was good, between the great wars of our century. He went originally in the first of the two wars and stayed until the coming of the second sent him home to a religious inheritance and to an America he had all but forgotten. Those two things, gifts of birth not understood until maturity, were the other elements in the formation of Rattner as artist.

He was born in Poughkeepsie, on the Hudson, in 1895, the son of an immigrant rabbinical student turned baker in flight from the violent anti-Semitism of Czarist Russia. The family was poor but infused with the traditional love of learning heightened, in America, by the recognition of learning as the key to the future. Rattner graduated from Poughkeepsie High School and enrolled in architecture at George Washington University in the nation's capital. He also began taking night courses at the nearby Corcoran School of Art, where he soon became a full-time art student, drawing extensively from life and attending an anatomy course at a Washington medical school. He transferred to the Pennsylvania Academy of the Fine Arts but was there only a year when World War I involved America. Rattner entered the Army and became a sergeant in camouflage, under the command of Homer Saint-Gaudens.

Camouflage was a fairly new military specialty when Rattner took it up, although, in one form or another, it had been prac-ticed for centuries, as by Malcolm's leaf-fringed army marching from Birnam Wood to Dunsinane. But in 1917 aerial observation changed the game completely. Rattner says that his principal job was ''chasing shadows'' early and late in the day, when the horizontal rays of the sun destroyed camouflage effects created for daylight. The style of World War I camouflage, of course, as old photographs attest, was right out of the contemporary art of Paris, involved as it was with the breaking up of forms and the development of abstract patterns. Perhaps more than most artists in military service, Rattner engaged in work closely related to his course of art studies. During the second Battle of the Marne, in the Chateau-Thiery sector, Rattner invented, as a kind of feint before the attack, a system for using life-size silhouettes in action positions. In that battle, he was injured by artillery fire and came home to America with a permanently lame back.

He returned to the Pennsylvania Academy long enough to win a Cresson traveling fellowship, with which he went back to Paris. There followed two mostly grim decades of intensive study, of daily poverty, of being dependent on his wife's earnings as a fashion reporter, and of lack of acceptance. He was a student, at different times, at the Ecole des Beaux-Arts, the Grand Chaumière, the Acadèmie Ranson and others, under such teachers as Bourdelle, Maurice Denis, Paul Sérusier and Roger Bissière. At least as important was his total absorption of the lessons of the Louvre and the other museums, where he studied with special attention the works of Rembrandt, Goya and Daumier.

Early in this Paris period he encountered Monet. With a few artist friends, he moved down the river to Giverny, where they raised potatoes, ate some and sold the rest for paint and canvas. He hid in the shrub fence beyond which Monet was painting his lily pond pictures and ''watched him swing that brush from the shoulder with the movement of a peasant farmer using the long-handled blade on the golden August harvest.'' Rattner relates that, once, while he was watching, a cloud momentarily obscured the sun. Monet shook his brush at the sky, which had so thoughtlessly destroyed his light patterns, and shouted, "Merde!"

Back in Paris, Rattner had broken-down studios in both Montmartre and Montparnasse. In one of them the roof was so bad that he found himself painting in the rain, protecting himself and his work with an umbrella. In 1924 he married Bettina Bedwell, a syndicated fashion writer. The gradual perfection of a personal style proceeded slowly, with only a very occasional sale of a painting to a collector. It was 1935, when Rattner was 40, that he had his first one-man show, at the Galerie Bonjean. The exhibition was not a commercial success, but Rattner remembers with affection the banquet his friends organized for the occasion. The government did buy a painting, *The Card Party*, for the Jeu de Paume, and that fall the painter had his first New York exhibition, at the Julien Levy Gallery.

In those last years of Paris residence, Rattner perfected his own mature style, one which was related to Cubism, Surrealism and Expressionism but which stood finally apart from all movements, from all systems of painting. He distorted figures freely into a severe angularity measured, sometimes, by black lines and illumined with thick, glowing colors. Such a description inevitably recalls Rouault and there were certainly points of contact between that French artist and the younger American one, but the differences were more profound than the likenesses.

In those years, too, the ancient German menace was rising once more in the east and bringing with it the note that Rattner's father had heard and fled from so long before in Russia. Listening to Hitler on the radio, Rattner became convinced that Europe would soon be no place for an artist and especially no place for a Jewish artist. He left for home in 1940, getting out of Paris before the Nazis got in and losing, in the process, a collection of his paintings representing 20 years of work and which have never been recovered. At this point, for the converging reasons of apparent failure at his profession and the mounting public urgency of world politics, Rattner was just about ready, or so he thought, to abandon art. It seemed to him that the most sensible thing he could do was to get a job in an American munitions factory in support of the battle of Britain and the future liberation of the continent.

Before doing so, however, he agreed to accompany his old friend Henry Miller, the novelist, on a voyage of rediscovery of America. The country obviously had changed enormously between the wars and the artist was filled with curiosity about the home to which he had returned. They went by car and their joint report on the country in prose and drawings is one of the basic documents of America just before the epochal change of World War II.

Rattner once said of his encounter with Monet that, "M. Monet discovered me just as I was discovering him," referring to the hedge-hiding surveillance of the Impressionist by the American. The same mutual discovery happened with his native country. Even as the artist, with Miller, was discovering America, so America, as France had never done, suddenly discovered Rattner as an artist. In another sense, too, an act of discovery took place and Rattner opened his art to the American experience of great spaces and crowds of people and empty worlds. Soon, there was a Rattner show in New York. Then, the Metropolitan Museum held an exhibition in which he was awarded the gold medal. He entered into the aesthetic life of New York and brought his own contribution to the European experience that younger New York painters were absorbing from artists-in-exile. There was no more talk about giving up art.

America has continued to be good to her native returned. Rattner has exhibited widely and his works are in the collections of most major museums. He has been invited to serve as artist in residence at two midwestern state universities and at the American Academy in Rome. He has taught at the Art Students' League and briefly conducted his own school at

Sag Harbor, Long Island. For the last fifteen years or so, he has regularly received commissions for large mural work in paint, stained glass, mosaic and tapestry.

Bettina Rattner died in 1947. In 1949 the artist married Esther Gentle, the sculptor, who is one of the most knowledgeable artists of the time in the techniques of printmaking. Their collaboration has resulted in a series of blazing, gorgeous prints carrying all the fervor and flame of Rattner's paintings.

The Rattners now divide their time among studios in Greenwich Village, in Sag Harbor and in Paris.

In the last years in France, Rattner had frequently painted religious scenes and objects. There is a particularly glowing painting of a country chapel, for instance, and he pictured the Nazi sweep into France as fire from heaven descending upon the Gothic cathedrals. But after absorbing that experience and the even deeper shock of the war's ending in the fire-cloud over Hiroshima, Rattner rediscovered the prophets and the sacred events of the religion of his fathers, the Judaism for which Herman Rattner had left his native land and which he had taught his son.

Rattner writes in journals and letters to friends in a free, loose manner expressive of the flow of thought and emotion. Here is a passage explaining the origin of a very large painting of the postwar years, *The Last Judgement:*

"The nightmare of Hiroshima-Nagasaki got me started—but the war was over—no, the war was not over—no, the war *is* not over. Maybe it's the way of civilization to have the air filled with the torment, anxieties, fears, doubts . . . Me and mine. You and yours . . . Always more, more, more. Do you have to dominate? Do you have to be the largest, the greatest, the biggest, the best? Always on and on . . . to the inevitable violence, collision, war, the sinister end. Haunted by a nightmare, the vision stares at my silence. . . . The painting becomes the interpretation of the final reality of the atom . . . the form and the color become the apocalyptic metaphors."

The war, then, in its beginning and in its ending shocked Rattner into the discovery of the people of the Book, a group which, for him, has always included Jesus, the prophet scorned and hung on a cross to die. He has painted Job, the man of faith who endured and remained steadfast in his faith through all suffering. He has painted Moses, the great leader of the Exodus from Egypt to the Promised Land of Israel. One moment in the pilgrimage of Moses has had special significance for Rattner, for he has painted it repeatedly. This is that moment of recognition on the mountain when God spoke to Moses from the flames of the burning bush, saying, "I am who am," and the prayer still repeated, "Hear O Israel, the Lord thy God, the Lord is One!" Rattner has painted the flames of the burning bush forming the Hebrew letters of these words of God.

But if many of his paintings since his return to America have been specific meditations on themes from scripture, it is also true that many of his paintings of subjects not overtly religious nevertheless carry a forceful presence that compels their acceptance as sacred images. Rattner has created a religious imagery of his own over the last three decades, one derived from his own deepening faith in the sacredness of all things touched by man, the child of God. In this sense, Rattner, almost alone, has renewed the ancient tradition of religious art just when it has seemed all but dead in the world at large.

A special invention of Rattner's in this personal religious imagery has been that of *The Window Cleaner*, a metaphor for God as timely to our age as was the image of the shepherd in the agrarian world of the Old Testament. In several works, Rattner has presented the window cleaner laboring patiently

12

to clean away the grime of daily life so that we may see through the transparent surface to the light and color of the universe.

Again, in the 1954 painting, *Arrangement of Old Shoes,* the artist assembles a line of what are literally the lowest of human accoutrements. But the leather is allowed to reflect bright colors; the paint is applied with thickness; the ensemble takes on a much more permanent implication than we think of, usually, in connection with the subject. These shoes have taken the imprint of the human foot in its daily journeys; they are therefore sacred and they are painted thus, almost like relics in the old religions. We recall the shoes of Vincent Van Gogh and of the little tramp of Charlie Chaplin. We recall the endless, tiring footsteps that compose a life.

In the Mirror, of 1961, employs a theme of the late Middle Ages and the Renaissance, one memorably painted by Picasso in our century. Here the contrast between reality and reflection is carried entirely by the paint qualities of the two images, the one on the left appearing thicker and more substantial.

Figures in the Market, 1966, has a ritual air about it, too, with the butcher emerging from darkness to hold up the bright red meat that gives its color to his hand in contrast to the dim, blue-veiled figure on the right. In pictures such as this, Rattner's language of paint—its complete command of the nuances of thick and thin, of color in darkness, of stains, smears and even drips—produces, rather surprisingly, an effect similar to that of the hieratic reverence of Byzantine mosaic.

The tragic irony that permeates Rattner's scribbled writings casts its light upon *The Red Carpet,* 1964. Against the faintly luminous blue of the background, the bright diagonal of the carpet, traditional city symbol of respect, contains the casual corpse of city violence, covered with newspapers. Rattner, in recent years, has added collage to his language of paint as simply part of the means available to the artistic vision. Here, real newspaper fragments are expertly cut and folded and affixed so as to bridge the world of the painting and the world of the spectator. In the French newsprint we discern a "Personals" column and a leading article "Against Hunger."

In 1952, Rattner became artist-in-residence at the University of Illinois, at Champagne-Urbana, in the rich, flat, farm country of downstate Illinois. The experience opened a new world of landscape to Rattner's art and he has painted it often. *Farmscape with Figures,* 1955, is a superb example. The thickly built up red paint, laid on in broad horizontal bands, is the prairie at sunset, soaked in the color of the dying sun, endless in its extent, broken here and there by buildings or figures that seem miniature against the sweep of the land.

A different kind of landscape is seen in *My Country, 'Tis of Thee,* 1967. Fragments of figures and faces dot the red and purple ground. A clown holds the sheet music of the title. A girl is seen. There is a fringe above the center section of evergreen needles, one made, it is seen on close inspection, of collage. The whole is a considered statement on the America that helped so much in the final molding of Rattner as an artist. There is great beauty, great expanse, some despair and, in the evergreen, always the hope of survival through whatever winter brings.

The clown figure who holds the sheet music in that song of America appears more fully developed in *The Painter,* of the same year. The clown, here, is the artist himself and the clown's face is tragic, not comic. The canvas within the canvas is painted deep red. Against it the purple suit of the painter glows and we see the edge of the canvas tacked to the stretcher. On the canvas three agonized figures are displayed. The clown-painter holds his brush aloft as if it were a flame and the whole picture is full of smoldering brilliances. The palette, which overlaps the canvas at the bottom, seems itself a painted mask.

14

The artist, assaying his own work, sees it, finally, as mere playacting against the world's agony he depicts.

It is not playacting that engages Abraham Rattner. At a time when artists were chiefly concerned with the development of their own art, Rattner rose out of that concern into a lasting passion for the agony and the beauty of the human situation. At a time when artists often seem to have abandoned everything for the sake of technique as an end in itself, Rattner continues with his deeply human concern, expressing it in a technique that has all the possibilities of painting at its command, one that moves freely among them to create from them a profound and enduring image of man on the earth.

Frank Getlein

Our civilization has become so complex that we often feel that we are living in a world of chaos and disorder.

All of the artists in this exhibition through their individual styles have given a poetic vision and sense of order to nature and man.

The Kennedy Galleries in this and future exhibitions will continue its policy of offering its clients a selection of quality paintings which reflect highly personal observations about man and his spirit.

RUDOLF G. WUNDERLICH
LAWRENCE A. FLEISCHMAN

CATALOGUE

3. FIGURE—BLUE AND RED, 1950
   oil on canvas; 36 x 28 inches

20

7. FARMSCAPE WITH FIGURES, 1955
   oil on canvas; 28¾ x 36½ inches

8. PRAIRIE SKY #3, 1955
   oil on canvas; 23½ x 38¾ inches

9. GARGOYLES #3, PARIS, 1959
    oil on canvas; 45 x 34 inches

10. GARGOYLES #3, GOTHIC, 1960
    oil on canvas; 48 x 36 inches

11. FIGURE IN FLAMES, 1961
oil on canvas; 51 ¼ x 38 inches

13. IN THE MIRROR #3, 1961
    oil on wood; 39 x 32 inches

14. VISION OF EZEKIAL, 1962
    oil on canvas; 51 x 77 inches

15. INTO THE NIGHT, 1962
    oil on canvas; 39 x 31 inches

19. MEAT CUTTER, 1964
   oil on canvas; 36¼ x 28¾ inches

21. THE CLOWN, 1964
     oil on canvas; 51 x 38 inches

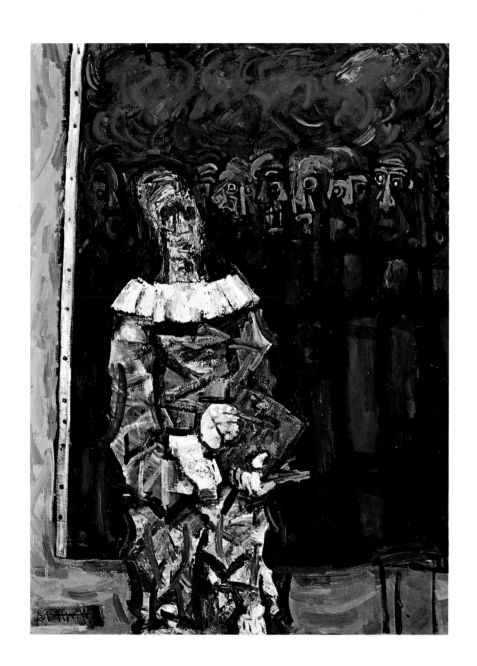

25. JUDAS MACCABBEUS, 1966
watercolor and ink; 16 x 12 inches

PAINTINGS IN THE EXHIBITION

1. GHOST CITY, 1941
   oil on canvas; 23 x 28 inches

2. FARM COMPOSITION #2, 1950
   oil on canvas; 46 x 35 inches

3. FIGURE—BLUE AND RED, 1950*
   oil on canvas; 36 x 28 inches

4. FIGURE WITH FISHING NET, 1951
   oil on canvas; 39¼ x 32 inches

5. WINDOW CLEANER, 1953
   oil on panel; 45¾ x 33¼ inches

6. OLD SHOES ARRANGEMENT #5, 1954
   oil on canvas; 25¾ x 32 inches

7. FARMSCAPE WITH FIGURES, 1955*
   oil on canvas; 28¾ x 36½ inches

8. PRAIRIE SKY #3, 1955*
   oil on canvas; 23½ x 38¾ inches

9. GARGOYLES #3, PARIS, 1959*
   oil on canvas; 45 x 34 inches

10. GARGOYLES #3, GOTHIC, 1960*
    oil on canvas; 48 x 36 inches

11. FIGURE IN FLAMES, 1961*
    oil on canvas; 51¼ x 38 inches

12. SEA STORM #1, 1961
    oil on canvas; 28 x 36 inches

13. IN THE MIRROR #3, 1961*
    oil on wood; 39 x 32 inches

14. VISION OF EZEKIAL, 1962*
    oil on canvas; 51 x 77 inches

15. INTO THE NIGHT, 1962*
    oil on canvas; 39 x 31 inches

*Illustrated.   (Continued)

PAINTINGS IN THE EXHIBITION

16. HOMAGE TO GOYA, 1963
    oil on canvas; 77 x 51 inches

17. STILL LIFE—THE CHOPPING BLOCK, 1963
    oil on canvas; 45¾ x 35 inches

18. FOUR OF THE JURY, 1964
    oil on canvas; 25¾ x 31¾ inches

19. MEAT CUTTER, 1964*
    oil on canvas; 36¼ x 28¾ inches

20. HAPPY BATHERS, 1964
    oil on canvas; 28¾ x 36¼ inches

21. THE CLOWN, 1964*
    oil on canvas; 51 x 38 inches

22. THE PAINTER, 1964
    oil on canvas; 57 x 38 inches

23. THE RED CARPET, 1964
    oil on canvas; 45 x 57 inches

24. SODOM AND GOMORRAH, 1965
    oil on canvas; 15 x 21½ inches

25. JUDAS MACCABBEUS, 1966*
    watercolor and ink; 16 x 12 inches

26. I HEAR AMERICA SINGING—WALT WHITMAN, 1966
    oil on panel; 34 x 46 inches

27. MAN WITH GUITAR, 1966
    oil on canvas; 39¼ x 32 inches

28. COMPOSITION IN RED AND GREEN WITH TWO FIGURES, 1967
    oil on canvas; 48 x 36 inches

29. FIGURES ON A TERRACE, 1967
    oil on canvas; 45 x 35 inches

30. PARADE, 1967
    oil on masonite; 45 x 57½ inches

31. NUDE SEATED NEAR THE RED DOOR, 1968
    oil on canvas; 36 x 30 inches

*Illustrated.

Index to Illustrations